"Enigmas of the Scientific and Riddly-5 Unleashed on

Embark on a thrilling journey through the world of science with "Enigmas of the Scientific World." This collection of 100 sets of captivating science riddles will test your knowledge, challenge your critical thinking, and ignite your curiosity about various scientific concepts. From exploring the mysteries of the universe to unraveling the secrets of the microscopic world, these riddles will engage and entertain both young and old minds alike. Get ready to unravel the enigmas and expand your scientific understanding through these intriguing puzzles. Whether you're a science enthusiast or simply enjoy a good riddle, this book will take you on an exciting adventure, revealing the wonders of the natural world and the marvels of scientific phenomena. Can you solve the riddles and unlock the secrets hidden within the realms of science? Find out in "Enigmas of the Scientific World." But the fun doesn't stop there! Indulge in a hilarious dose of laughter with "The Giggly-5 and Ridley-5." This collection of 100 sets of silly dad jokes about science will tickle your funny bone and leave you chuckling uncontrollably. With puns, wordplay, and quirky humor, these jokes explore various scientific concepts in the most amusing way. From the whimsical antics of atoms to the wacky world of physics, these jokes are perfect for entertaining both kids and adults. Turn learning science into a giggle-filled experience with "The Giggly-5 and Riddly-5."

Prepare yourself for a delightful journey filled with laughter, curiosity, groans, and giggles as you delve into the comical side of the scientific world. Let the Giggly-5 and Ridley-5 tickle your funny bone with their pun-tastic humor and witty wordplay. Expand your scientific knowledge, solve mind-bending riddles, and share a laugh with family and friends. It's time for a rib-tickling science adventure like no other!

If you like the book, please review us at Amazon

Riddly-5: The Mysterious Attraction

Clue	Problem
1.	I have two poles, North and South, attracting or repelling with no mouth.
2.	My force can pull objects together, but only if they are made of certain materials.
3.	I am a crucial component of compasses, helping people find their way.
4.	I can induce electric current in wires, allowing for the creation of electricity.
5.	What am I?

Answer: Magnet

Giggly-5

1. Why was the math book feeling down? Because it had too many problems!

2. How does the moon cut his hair? Eclipse it!

3. Why was the computer cold? It left its Windows open!

4. Why was the microscope good at making decisions? Because it could always see the bigger picture!

5. Why did the photon refuse to check a suitcase at the airport? Because it was traveling light!

Riddly-5: The Sparkling Celestial Body

Clue	Problem
1.	I am a massive ball of hot, glowing gases, shining in the sky.
2.	I provide heat and light to the planets in my solar system.
3.	I am composed mostly of hydrogen and helium.
4.	My energy is produced through nuclear fusion.
5.	What am I?

Answer: Star

Giggly-5

1. Why did the scientist bring a pencil to the lab? In case he wanted to draw some conclusions!

2. Why was the cell so good at social media? It had lots of followers on its cell-wall!

3. How does a physicist exercise? By pumping ion!

4. What do you call a microbiologist who's just moved to a new city? A germ settler!

5. What do astronomers put on their toast? Space Jam!

Riddly-5: The Energetic Powerhouse

Clue	Problem
1.	I am the "powerhouse" of the cell, generating energy for its functions.
2.	I have a double membrane and my own DNA.
3.	I am responsible for converting nutrients into ATP, the cell's main energy source.
4.	Muscle cells contain a large number of me.
5.	What am I?

Answer: Mitochondrion

Giggly-5

1. Why did the chemist sit on a whoopee cushion? Because he wanted to cause a reaction!

2. Why did the geologist take his girlfriend to the quarry? Because he wanted to show her a gneiss time!

3. What did the DNA say to the RNA? "Stop copying me!"

4. Why do biologists look forward to Casual Friday? Because they get to wear genes to work!

5. Why do mathematicians hate the U.S. Midwest? Too many plains!

Riddly-5: The Invisible Force

Clue	Problem
1.	I am a fundamental force of nature, always present but unseen.
2.	I am responsible for the attraction between all objects with mass.
3.	My strength depends on the masses of the objects and the distance between them.
4.	I keep celestial bodies, like planets, in orbit around their stars.
5.	What am I?

Answer: Gravity

Giggly-5

1. What did the excited gardener do when he discovered a new plant species? He soiled his plants!

2. What does an anatomist do when she's unsure about a body part? She goes with her gut!

3. Why did the neurologist break up with the brain? It had too many mind games!

4. What do physicists enjoy cooking the most? Fission chips!

5. Why did the chemistry lab explode? Too much solution!

Riddly-5: The Building Blocks of Life

Clue	Problem
1.	I am the basic unit of life, the smallest part that can carry out all the functions of an organism.
2.	I contain genetic information in the form of DNA.
3.	I can be found in a variety of shapes and sizes, from simple to complex.
4.	Cells are made up of many of me, each with a specific role.
5.	What am I?

Answer: Cell

Giggly-5

1. Why was the computer always tired when it got home? It had a hard drive!

2. Why did the astronaut break up with his girlfriend? He needed space!

3. What's a physicist's favorite part of a baseball game? The wave!

4. Why did the botanist leave the party early? He wasn't feeling very plantastic!

5. Why don't mathematicians get sunburned? They use sine block!

Riddly-5: The Fastest Force in the Universe

Clue	Problem
1.	I am the fastest force in the universe, capable of traveling at approximately 300,000 kilometers per second.
2.	I am made up of particles called photons.
3.	I can travel through empty space, as well as transparent materials like air and glass.
4.	I am responsible for the sensation of sight.
5.	What is this force that travels at incredible speed?

Answer: Light

Giggly-5

1. Why don't biologists like fast food? They can't catch it under the microscope!
2. Why did the math teacher get a ladder? To reach new heights!
3. What did the proton say to the electron? Stop being so negative!
4. Why was the robot on a diet? He had too many bytes!
5. How does a scientist freshen her breath? With experi-mints!

Riddly-5: The Great Balance Keeper

Clue	Problem
1.	I am a force that keeps objects in balance and prevents them from falling.
2.	I am caused by the interaction between an object's mass and the force of gravity.
3.	I allow birds to perch on branches and humans to walk without falling.
4.	A tightrope walker relies on me to stay balanced while crossing a thin rope.
5.	What is this force that keeps objects steady and prevents them from toppling over?

Answer: Stability

Giggly-5

1. Why did the biologist go to the bar? To study the "cell"ular structure!

2. Why did the astronomer bring a ladder to work? He wanted to reach for the stars!

3. Why did the math book go to therapy? It had too many problems to solve!

4. What do you call a physicist who catches fish? A Hook's Law!

5. Why don't computers take their coffee with sugar? They like it on the hard drive!

Riddly-5: The Mighty Fire Creator

Clue	Problem
1.	I am a chemical reaction that releases heat, light, and often produces a flame.
2.	I require three main ingredients: fuel, oxygen, and heat.
3.	I have been used by humans for cooking, heating, and various other purposes for thousands of years.
4.	I am a rapid oxidation process that produces energy in the form of heat and light.
5.	What is this process that creates fire and provides warmth and light?

Answer: Combustion

Giggly-5

1. Why do biologists like multi-level marketing schemes? They love cell multiplication!

2. How did the mathematician solve his constipation problem? He worked it out with a pencil!

3. Why did the weather forecaster bring a bar of soap to work? He wanted a clean forecast!

4. What do you call two birds in love? Tweet-hearts!

5. Why did the chemist like working with ammonia? It was pretty basic stuff!

Riddly-5: The Protective Force Field

Clue	Problem
1.	I am a natural protective layer surrounding the Earth.
2.	I shield the planet from harmful solar radiation and charged particles.
3.	I extend from about 80 kilometers above the Earth's surface to hundreds of kilometers in height.
4.	I have different regions called the ionosphere, exosphere, and magnetosphere.
5.	What is this protective layer that keeps us safe from space radiation?

Answer: Atmosphere

Giggly-5

1. What does a geologist call his ex? A tectonic plate because they always split apart!

2. Why did the math problem look so sad? It had too many fractions to deal with!

3. Why was the computer cold? It left its Windows open!

4. Why did the botanist stay at home? He wanted to turn over a new leaf!

5. What do you call a single-celled organism that won't share its chocolate? A choco-mono-gate!

Riddly-5: The Color Spectrum

Clue	Problem
1.	I am the range of colors that can be seen when white light passes through a prism or is dispersed in droplets of water.
2.	I consist of seven main colors: red, orange, yellow, green, blue, indigo, and violet.
3.	Each color in me has a different wavelength and frequency.
4.	I can be observed in phenomena like rainbows, sunsets, and color spectrums produced by glass or water.
5.	What is this range of colors that brings beauty and vibrancy to our world?

Answer: Rainbow

Giggly-5

1. Why did the chemist keep smashing atoms together? He was trying to crack the code!

2. Why did the fish study marine biology? It wanted to know more about its school!

3. What do you call a physicist who's been knighted? Sir Round!

4. Why did the computer go to art school? It wanted to improve its graphics!

5. Why was the calculator a great musician? It knew the keys!

Riddly-5: The Master of Adaptation

Clue	Problem
1.	I am a process through which organisms change and adjust to their environment over time.
2.	I am driven by genetic variations and the process of natural selection.
3.	I allow species to develop traits that increase their chances of survival and reproduction.
4.	I can lead to the formation of new species over long periods of time.
5.	What is this process that enables organisms to thrive in changing environments?

Answer: Evolution

Giggly-5

1. Why did the microorganism refuse to play cards with the jungle cat? Because he was afraid of cheetahs!

2. Why did the botanist always carry a map? He didn't want to get lost in the woods!

3. What do you call an acid with an attitude? A mean-o-acid!

4. What did the parallel lines say to the intersecting lines? "You've crossed a line!"

5. Why did the computer go to school? It wanted to improve its processing skills!

Riddly-5: The Building Blocks of Matter

Clue	Problem
1.	I am the smallest unit of a chemical element, representing its unique properties.
2.	I consist of a nucleus containing protons and neutrons, surrounded by electrons.
3.	I combine to form molecules and compounds.
4.	I have different types, each with a unique number of protons.
5.	What are these fundamental particles that make up all matter?

Answer: Atoms

Giggly-5

1. Why did the biologist bring a pencil to the lab? To draw blood!

2. Why was the math teacher overweight? Because she loved pi!

3. What do you call an astronomer who tells bad jokes? A shooting star!

4. Why was the computer in school? It was learning its bytes!

5. What's a biologist's favorite board game? Organ-Trail!

Riddly-5: The Heavenly Body that Orbits the Earth

Clue	Problem
1.	I am a celestial body that orbits the Earth.
2.	I can be natural or artificial.
3.	I provide communication, navigation, and weather data.
4.	Some of the famous ones include Hubble, GPS, and ISS.
5.	What am I?

Answer: Satellite

Giggly-5

1. Why did the cell go to prison? Because it had bad cell behavior!

2. Why was the physics book so good at the gym? It had excellent 'workout' problems!

3. Why did the computer break up with its partner? It was done processing!

4. What did the botanist say at the funeral? "We have to photosynthesize with the family."

5. Why did the number 7 get a time-out? It was too mean to 9!

Riddly-5: The Force Behind Earth's Weather

Clue	Problem
1.	I am the force that drives Earth's weather patterns.
2.	I am caused by the unequal heating of the Earth's surface.
3.	I create wind, storms, and other atmospheric phenomena.
4.	I am influenced by factors such as temperature, humidity, and air pressure.
5.	What is this force that determines our daily weather conditions?

Answer: Wind

Giggly-5

1. Why did the chemist like ironing clothes? Because it was a smoothing operator!

2. Why don't astronomers get lost at night? They always look up!

3. What do you call an angry computer? A byte-r!

4. Why did the scientist install a knocker on his door? He wanted to win the no-bell prize!

5. Why was the math test so sad? Because its problems were never solved!

Riddly-5: The Liquid of Life

Clue	Problem
1.	I am a transparent, odorless, and tasteless substance.
2.	I am essential for all known forms of life.
3.	I can exist in three states: solid, liquid, and gas.
4.	I cover approximately 71% of the Earth's surface.
5.	What am I?

Answer: Water

Giggly-5

1. What did the biologist wear to his first date? Designer genes!

2. Why did the atom go to the party alone? Because it couldn't find anyone to bond with!

3. Why did the computer go to the doctor? It had a virus!

4. Why don't trees use computers? They're afraid of logging in!

5. Why don't mathematicians get cold? Because they have so many layers!

Riddly-5: The Powerful Force of Nature

Clue	Problem
1.	I am a natural disaster that occurs when the Earth's lithosphere experiences sudden and violent movement.
2.	I can cause shaking of the ground, destruction of buildings, and even tsunamis.
3.	I am measured using a seismograph and can have different magnitudes.
4.	I am caused by the release of energy in the Earth's crust.
5.	What is this powerful force that can shape landscapes in an instant?

Answer: Earthquake

Giggly-5

1. Why did the photon break up with the electron? It was tired of being taken for light!

2. What's an astronaut's favorite exercise? Moonwalks!

3. Why don't computers go on dates? They prefer networking!

4. Why did the math problem go to therapy? It had too many unresolved issues!

5. Why did the scientist take out his doorbell? He wanted to win the no-bell prize!

Riddly-5: The Marvelous Molecular Builders

Clue	Problem
1.	We are the fundamental units that make up all living organisms.
2.	We are large, complex molecules composed of chains of amino acids.
3.	We have diverse functions, including serving as enzymes, hormones, and structural components.
4.	Our unique sequence determines the characteristics and traits of an organism.
5.	What are we?

Answer: Proteins

Giggly-5

1. Why did the atom split up with its partner? It couldn't handle the bond anymore!
2. Why did the galaxy get an award? Because it had outstanding stars!
3. What did the computer do at lunchtime? Had a byte!
4. What do you call a fish made out of 2 sodium atoms? 2 Na!
5. Why was the math book so arrogant? It had all the solutions!

Riddly-5: The Power Source of the Cell

Clue	Problem
1.	I am a tiny, rod-shaped organelle found in the cells of all living organisms.
2.	I am often called the "powerhouse of the cell" because I produce energy.
3.	I am responsible for converting food molecules into usable energy in the form of ATP.
4.	I have my own set of DNA and can reproduce independently within the cell.
5.	What am I?

Answer: Mitochondria

Giggly-5

1. Why did the gene go to therapy? It felt manipulated by genetic engineers!

2. Why was the math equation so happy at the party? Because it got squared away!

3. What did the hard drive say to the CPU? You spin me right round!

4. Why was the botanist always broke? Because he always leaves his money in the bush!

5. Why do chemists like high pH solutions? Because they can't resist a basic instinct!

Riddly-5: The Invisible Gas We Breathe

Clue	Problem
1.	I am a colorless, odorless gas that is essential for the survival of all living organisms.
2.	I make up approximately 78% of the Earth's atmosphere.
3.	I am necessary for the process of respiration in plants and animals.
4.	I can combine with other elements to form compounds like water and carbon dioxide.
5.	What is this invisible gas we breathe?

Answer: Oxygen

Giggly-5

1. Why do biologists make great comedians? Because they know all the organ-ic jokes!

2. Why did the lightbulb fail the physics test? It wasn't too bright!

3. What's a computer's favorite snack? Microchips!

4. Why was the plant at the police station? It was picked up for photosynthesizing!

5. Why did the mathematician bring a ladder to class? Because he wanted to reach higher equations!

Riddly-5: The Microscopic Powerhouses

Clue	Problem
1.	We are small, membrane-bound organelles found in the cells of plants and algae.
2.	We are the sites of photosynthesis, a process that converts sunlight into chemical energy.
3.	We contain chlorophyll, a pigment that captures light energy.
4.	We produce oxygen as a byproduct of photosynthesis.
5.	What are we?

Answer: Chloroplasts

Giggly-5

1. Why don't chemists trust atoms? Because they make up everything!
2. Why did the galaxy get a timeout? It wouldn't stop revolving around itself!
3. Why was the computer cold? It left its Windows open!
4. Why did the flower go to school? To grow its budding intellect!
5. Why did the equation go to therapy? It felt unequal!

Riddly-5: The Nature's Architects

Clue	Problem
1.	We are tiny creatures that build intricate structures using materials from our surroundings.
2.	Our constructions can vary from simple nests to complex hives and webs.
3.	We play a crucial role in pollination, seed dispersal, and ecosystem balance.
4.	Some of us are solitary, while others live in colonies or societies.
5.	What are we?

Answer: Insects

Giggly-5

1. Why did the cell phone go to school? It wanted to improve its data analysis!

2. Why do physicists love baseball? Because it's full of field theories!

3. Why did the scientist bring a ladder into the lab? He wanted to reach for the stars!

4. What's a tree's favorite mathematical function? Logarithms!

5. Why did the math problem look so sad? Because of its complex roots!

Riddly-5: The Secret Chemical Messengers

Clue	Problem
1.	We are chemical messengers produced by the endocrine glands in the body.
2.	We regulate various bodily functions, including growth, metabolism, and reproduction.
3.	Imbalances in our production or release can lead to hormonal disorders.
4.	Our effects can be widespread, influencing physical and emotional well-being.
5.	What are we?

Answer: Hormones

Giggly-5

1. What do you call a nervous java coder? A "Java-lin"!

2. Why was the planet so humble? It knew it wasn't the center of the universe!

3. Why did the biologist go to the dance? To see the "e-motion"!

4. Why did the mathematician always bring a compass to parties? He wanted to have a good "point"!

5. Why did the chemistry experiment feel so depressed? It had a poor reaction!

Riddly-5: The Brilliant Source of Energy

Clue	Problem
1.	I am a process that involves the conversion of light energy into chemical energy.
2.	I occur in green plants, algae, and some bacteria.
3.	I require chlorophyll and sunlight to take place.
4.	I produce glucose, which serves as a source of energy for the organism.
5.	What am I?

Answer: Photosynthesis

Giggly-5

1. Why did the botanist go on a date with a vine? Because he wanted to see a new "leaf"!

2. Why was the computer scientist always happy? Because he found joy in "coding"!

3. What do you call a scientist who loves fizzy drinks? A "physi-soda"!

4. Why did the mathematician call his dog "Pi"? Because it was irrational and went on and on!

5. Why did the physics teacher break up with the biology teacher? Because they had no "chemistry"!

Riddly-5: The Earth's Protective Shield

Clue	Problem
1.	I am a layer of gases that surrounds the Earth.
2.	I protect the planet from harmful ultraviolet radiation from the Sun.
3.	I consist mainly of oxygen, nitrogen, and traces of other gases.
4.	I play a vital role in regulating the Earth's temperature.
5.	What am I?

Answer: Ozone Layer

Giggly-5

1. Why did the computer become a tour guide? It had a great memory for routes and details!

2. Why did the chemist start a wine bar? He knew all about fermentation!

3. Why did the tree become a therapist? It was great at listening and staying grounded!

4. Why did the equation start a podcast? It wanted to talk about the problems that matter!

5. Why did the scientist become a bartender? He was curious about the chemistry of cocktails!

Riddly-5: The Life-Sustaining Liquid in Plants

Clue	Problem
1.	I am a liquid that is essential for the survival of plants.
2.	I am transported through specialized tissues in the plant.
3.	I provide nutrients and water to different parts of the plant.
4.	I play a role in maintaining turgidity and structure in plant cells.
5.	What am I?

Answer: Sap

Giggly-5

1. Why did the silicon atom start dating the oxygen atom? Because it had an "electronegative" attraction!

2. Why did the botanist have a secret crush on the palm tree? Because she was frond of him!

3. Why don't programmers like nature? Because it has too many bugs!

4. Why was the number Pi feeling low? It was feeling irrational!

5. Why did the astronomer break up with the star? Because it was always burning him!

Riddly-5: The Energetic Particle Accelerator

Clue	Problem
1.	I am a device that accelerates charged particles to high speeds.
2.	I am used for scientific research, medical imaging, and cancer treatment.
3.	I can create intense beams of electrons, protons, or ions.
4.	I work on the principle of electromagnetic fields and electric potentials.
5.	What am I?

Answer: Particle Accelerator

Giggly-5

1. Why did the biologists go to the bar? They wanted to have a "cell"-ebration!

2. What do you call a group of musical chemists? A band of "ions"!

3. Why did the computer go broke? Because it had too many bytes!

4. Why was the flower always broke? Because it kept "petaling" away its money!

5. Why was the math teacher's son bad at math? Because he wouldn't count on his father's help!

Riddly-5: The Universal Solvent

Clue	Problem
1.	I am a chemical substance that has the ability to dissolve many other substances.
2.	I am essential for various biological processes, such as digestion and transportation of nutrients.
3.	I have a high heat capacity, allowing me to absorb and release heat slowly.
4.	I am neutral, neither acidic nor basic, with a pH of 7.
5.	What am I?

Answer: Water

Giggly-5

1. Why was the astronaut a good gardener? Because he had plenty of space!

2. Why did the computer start sneezing? It caught a virus!

3. Why did the plant get in trouble at school? It kept leaving during biology class!

4. Why was the math teacher a good farmer? He knew how to square roots!

5. Why did the biologist bring a turtle to the party? He wanted to come out of his shell!

Riddly-5: The Genetic Blueprint

Clue	Problem
1.	I am a molecule that carries the genetic information of an organism.
2.	I have a double helix structure made up of nucleotides.
3.	I contain the instructions for building and maintaining an organism.
4.	I can be replicated and passed down from one generation to another.
5.	What am I?

Answer: DNA

Giggly-5

1. Why did the scientist become a gardener? He wanted to see his plants grow organically!

2. Why was the computer so high in demand? Because it had all the right chips!

3. Why was the sun a good listener? It was always light years away!

4. Why did the botanist go to the flower shop? He wanted to pick up a blooming beauty!

5. Why did the equation look upset? It couldn't figure out its X!

Riddly-5: The Miraculous Plant Food Factory

Clue	Problem
1.	I am a process by which green plants convert light energy into chemical energy.
2.	I occur in chloroplasts and involve the synthesis of glucose.
3.	I require carbon dioxide, water, and light to take place.
4.	I produce oxygen as a byproduct.
5.	What am I?

Answer: Photosynthesis

Giggly-5

1. Why did the star refuse to join the galaxy? It wanted to twinkle alone!

2. Why did the computer go to the dance party? To get its groove back!

3. Why did the scientist take his dog to the lab? He wanted to study barkology!

4. Why did the mathematician bring a ruler to the party? He wanted to measure the fun!

5. Why was the periodic table always calm? Because it had a lot of elements under control!

Riddly-5: The Invisible Air We Breathe

Clue	Problem
1.	I am a mixture of gases that surrounds the Earth.
2.	I am essential for the survival of all living organisms.
3.	I consist mainly of nitrogen, oxygen, and small amounts of other gases.
4.	I can be compressed, expanded, and have pressure.
5.	What am I?

Answer: Atmosphere

Giggly-5

1. Why was the astronomer a bad player? He always lost his space!

2. Why did the computer visit the psychiatrist? It had a hard drive!

3. Why was the scientist's cat always happy? It was purr-iodically excited!

4. Why did the flower go to the dance party? To bust a blooming move!

5. Why was the math teacher a good sailor? He could always find the right angle!

Riddly-5: The Master of Camouflage

Clue	Problem
1.	I am an adaptation that allows an organism to blend into its surroundings.
2.	I help the organism hide from predators or ambush prey.
3.	I can involve changes in color, pattern, or texture.
4.	Some animals use me to mimic their environment.
5.	What am I?

Answer: Camouflage

Giggly-5

1. Why was the biology book so full of itself? It had all the "organ"ization!

2. Why did the planet go to school? It wanted to be a star!

3. Why did the computer get kicked off the football team? It had too many bytes!

4. Why did the tree go to the dentist? It had a root problem!

5. Why was the math book always unhappy? It had too many problems!

Riddly-5: The Electrical Messenger

Clue	Problem
1.	I am a specialized cell that transmits electrical signals in the body.
2.	I am the basic unit of the nervous system.
3.	I can transmit signals to and from the brain.
4.	I am responsible for coordinating movement, sensation, and other functions.
5.	What am I?

Answer: Neuron

Giggly-5

1. Why was the mushroom a good scientist? Because he was a fungi (fun guy)!

2. Why did the computer take its sunglasses to the beach? It didn't want to get a sun byte!

3. Why was the leaf a good mathematician? Because it always gets to the root of the problem!

4. Why was the geologist always relaxing? Because he takes life for granite!

5. Why did the scientist bring a pen to the lab? To draw blood!

Riddly-5: The Silent Nighttime Hunter

Clue	Problem
1.	I am a nocturnal predator known for my silent flight.
2.	I have exceptional hearing and can rotate my head almost 270 degrees.
3.	I am often associated with wisdom in folklore and mythology.
4.	I can be found in various habitats worldwide.
5.	What am I?

Answer: Owl

Giggly-5

1. Why did the computer go to the doctor? It had a bad case of CAPS LOCK!

2. Why did the atom cross the road? It was time to split!

3. Why did the scientist install a doorbell in his lab? Because he wanted to win the No-bell prize!

4. Why was the physicist bad at playing cards? Because he always tried to deal with the gravity of the situation!

5. Why was the algebra book always sad? It had too many problems to solve!

Riddly-5: The Spark of Life

Clue	Problem
1.	I am a tiny, membrane-bound structure found in all living cells.
2.	I am the site of cellular respiration, producing energy in the form of ATP.
3.	I have my own set of DNA, separate from the cell's nucleus.
4.	I can be found in large numbers in metabolically active cells.
5.	What am I?

Answer: Mitochondrion

Giggly-5

1. Why did the astronaut bring a broom into space? To clean up the stardust!

2. Why did the computer take a nap? It needed to reboot!

3. Why do chemists love coffee? Because it's always full of elements!

4. Why did the tree go to the barber? It needed a trim!

5. Why was the triangle always confused? It couldn't figure out which side to take!

Riddly-5: The Force Behind All Interactions

Clue	Problem
1.	I am a fundamental force of nature that governs all interactions between particles.
2.	I can attract or repel objects based on their charges.
3.	I play a crucial role in holding atoms and molecules together.
4.	I am responsible for the electrical and magnetic phenomena in the universe.
5.	What am I?

Answer: Electromagnetic Force

Giggly-5

1. Why was the computer always cold? It left its Windows open!

2. Why did the scientist go to the disco? To experiment with some funky moves!

3. Why was the flower a great poet? It had a budding talent!

4. Why did the calculator go to therapy? It had too many problems to solve!

5. Why was the botanist such a great artist? He knew how to draw a perfect petal!

Riddly-5: The Tiny Factories of Protein Synthesis

Clue	Problem
1.	I am a small cellular structure where proteins are synthesized.
2.	I can be found in the cytoplasm of all cells.
3.	I consist of RNA and protein molecules.
4.	I read the genetic instructions and assemble amino acids into proteins.
5.	What am I?

Answer: Ribosome

Giggly-5

1. Why did the computer refuse to play the video game? It was afraid of catching a bug!

2. Why did the atom go to the party solo? It didn't want to bond!

3. Why did the scientist carry a notebook everywhere? He had a theory that needed testing!

4. Why did the plant go to the bank? It wanted to start a grow account!

5. Why was the equation always calm? It always balanced itself out!

Riddly-5: The Giant of the Solar System

Clue	Problem
1.	I am the largest planet in our solar system.
2.	I have a prominent set of rings surrounding me.
3.	I am composed mostly of hydrogen and helium.
4.	I have a great red spot, a persistent storm, on my surface.
5.	What am I?

Answer: Jupiter

Giggly-5

1. Why was the computer's screen always bright? It refused to take a byte out of the apple!

2. Why did the chemist go to the cafe? He needed a strong solution!

3. Why did the tree refuse to play chess? It was a bad check-mate!

4. Why did the algebra equation look so happy? It found its X!

5. Why was the scientist always thirsty? He had an insatiable quest for knowledge!

Riddly-5: The Universal Force of Attraction

Clue	Problem
1.	I am a fundamental force that attracts objects with mass.
2.	I keep celestial bodies, like planets, in orbit around stars.
3.	I am responsible for the falling of objects on Earth.
4.	I have a force that depends on the masses of the objects and the distance between them.
5.	What am I?

Answer: Gravity

Giggly-5

1. Why did the computer join the music band? It had great chips and was great at processing beats!

2. Why was the chemist a great chef? He knew all the ingredients to the element!

3. Why did the tree love math? It was great with figures (and leaves)!

4. Why was the algebra book a great comedian? It could solve problems with a funny twist!

5. Why did the scientist love hiking? He loved to experiment with altitude!

Riddly-5: The Ocean's Liquid Fire

Clue	Problem
1.	I am a phenomenon of the ocean where the water appears to be on fire.
2.	I am caused by the presence of bioluminescent organisms.
3.	I often occur at night when the water is disturbed.
4.	I create a mesmerizing display of glowing light.
5.	What am I?

Answer: Bioluminescence

Giggly-5

1. Why did the computer go to art school? It wanted to learn how to draw on its tablet!

2. Why was the chemist always healthy? He had all the solutions to his problems!

3. Why did the plant love to party? It was always budding with excitement!

4. Why was the math book always popular? It had all the right angles!

5. Why did the scientist become a musician? He wanted to experiment with sound waves!

Riddly-5: The Spectacular Light Display in the Sky

Clue	Problem
1.	I am a natural light display that occurs in the polar regions.
2.	I am caused by the interaction between charged particles from the Sun and the Earth's atmosphere.
3.	I come in a variety of colors, including green, pink, and purple.
4.	I am best observed in dark, clear skies away from light pollution.
5.	What am I?

Answer: Aurora

Giggly-5

1. Why did the computer become a chef? It was excellent at data processing!

2. Why did the scientist become a rockstar? He was great at playing with different elements!

3. Why was the flower always the life of the party? It was always blooming!

4. Why did the calculator join the debate team? It always had a point to add!

5. Why was the geologist never lost? He always knew how to rock!

Riddly-5: The Master of Camouflage

Clue	Problem
1.	I am an adaptation that allows an organism to blend into its surroundings.
2.	I help the organism hide from predators or ambush prey.
3.	I can involve changes in color, pattern, or texture.
4.	Some animals use me to mimic their environment.
5.	Which adaptation allows an organism to blend into its surroundings?

Answer: Camouflage

Giggly-5

1. Why was the computer a great musician? It knew the keys!

2. Why was the chemist always relaxed? He knew all the elements of peace!

3. Why did the tree become a poet? It was good with words and even better with leaves!

4. Why did the algebra book go to the party? It knew how to multiply the fun!

5. Why did the scientist become a politician? He wanted to conduct an experiment in democracy!

Riddly-5: The Electrical Messenger

Clue	Problem
1.	I am a specialized cell that transmits electrical signals in the body.
2.	I am the basic unit of the nervous system.
3.	I can transmit signals to and from the brain.
4.	I am responsible for coordinating movement, sensation, and other functions.
5.	What is this specialized cell that transmits electrical signals in the body called?

Answer: Neuron

Giggly-5

1. Why did the computer become a detective? It could process clues faster!

2. Why did the chemist never get bored? He had all the elements of fun!

3. Why did the plant go to the casino? It was feeling lucky (chloro)fill!

4. Why was the math book always broke? It couldn't count on anyone!

5. Why did the scientist become a pilot? He wanted to defy gravity!

Riddly-5: The Silent Nighttime Hunter

Clue	Problem
1.	I am a nocturnal predator known for my silent flight.
2.	I have exceptional hearing and can rotate my head almost 270 degrees.
3.	I am often associated with wisdom in folklore and mythology.
4.	I can be found in various habitats worldwide.
5.	Which creature is known for its silent flight and exceptional hearing abilities?

Answer: Owl

Giggly-5

1. Why did the computer start a blog? It wanted to share its thoughts byte by byte!

2. Why was the chemist a great magician? He knew the trick to every element!

3. Why was the tree a great writer? It could turn over a new leaf every day!

4. Why did the calculator become a therapist? It was great at solving problems!

5. Why did the scientist become a baker? He wanted to experiment with yeast!

Riddly-5: The Spark of Life

Clue	Problem
1.	I am a tiny, membrane-bound structure found in all living cells.
2.	I am the site of cellular respiration, producing energy in the form of ATP.
3.	I have my own set of DNA, separate from the cell's nucleus.
4.	I can be found in large numbers in metabolically active cells.
5.	What is this tiny structure responsible for producing energy in the form of ATP?

Answer: Mitochondrion

Giggly-5

1. Why was the computer always the DJ at parties? It had all the best hard drives!

2. Why was the chemist good at poker? He knew all the elements of bluffing!

3. Why was the tree always calm? It knew how to stay grounded!

4. Why did the math equation join a band? It knew it could count on the rhythm!

5. Why did the scientist bring a ladder to work? He wanted to climb the ladder of success!

Riddly-5: The Force Behind All Interactions

Clue	Problem
1.	I am a fundamental force of nature that governs all interactions between particles.
2.	I can attract or repel objects based on their charges.
3.	I play a crucial role in holding atoms and molecules together.
4.	I am responsible for the electrical and magnetic phenomena in the universe.
5.	Which fundamental force governs all interactions between particles?

Answer: Electromagnetic Force

Giggly-5

1. Why did the computer go to the coffee shop? It needed a good java!

2. Why was the chemist a great dancer? He knew how to shake things up!

3. Why did the tree win the race? It always stayed rooted in one place!

4. Why did the algebra book get a job? It was good at solving for X!

5. Why did the scientist go to the gym? He wanted to exercise his hypotheses!

Riddly-5: The Tiny Factories of Protein Synthesis

Clue	Problem
1.	I am a small cellular structure where proteins are synthesized.
2.	I can be found in the cytoplasm of all cells.
3.	I consist of RNA and protein molecules.
4.	I read the genetic instructions and assemble amino acids into proteins.
5.	What is the name of the small cellular structure responsible for protein synthesis?

Answer: Ribosome

Giggly-5

1. Why was the computer always hired for jobs? It had excellent programming skills!

2. Why did the chemist open a bakery? He had a recipe for success!

3. Why did the plant go to the party? It was always up for a little photosynthesis fun!

4. Why did the calculator join the football team? It knew the score!

5. Why did the scientist go to the music concert? He was studying sound waves!

Riddly-5: The Giant of the Solar System

Clue	Problem
1.	I am the largest planet in our solar system.
2.	I have a prominent set of rings surrounding me.
3.	I am composed mostly of hydrogen and helium.
4.	I have a great red spot, a persistent storm, on my surface.
5.	Which planet is the largest in our solar system and has a prominent set of rings?

Answer: Jupiter

Giggly-5

1. Why did the computer go to the concert? It wanted to improve its sound card!

2. Why was the chemist always full? He had plenty of food for thought!

3. Why did the tree get the job? It had good references!

4. Why was the math book always organized? It kept everything in order!

5. Why did the scientist go to the beach? He wanted to study the waves!

Riddly-5: The Universal Force of Attraction

Clue	Problem
1.	I am a fundamental force that attracts objects with mass.
2.	I keep celestial bodies, like planets, in orbit around stars.
3.	I am responsible for the falling of objects on Earth.
4.	I have a force that depends on the masses of the objects and the distance between them.
5.	What is this fundamental force that attracts objects with mass?

Answer: Gravity

Giggly-5

1. Why did the computer join the circus? It wanted to juggle its tasks better!

2. Why was the chemist always happy? He had a positive reaction to everything!

3. Why did the tree join the choir? It had perfect pitch (pine)!

4. Why did the equation go to the zoo? It wanted to add some excitement to its life!

5. Why did the scientist go to the opera? He was studying the sound of music!

Riddly-5: The Ocean's Liquid Fire

Clue	Problem
1.	I am a phenomenon of the ocean where the water appears to be on fire.
2.	I am caused by the presence of bioluminescent organisms.
3.	I often occur at night when the water is disturbed.
4.	I create a mesmerizing display of glowing light.
5.	What is this phenomenon in the ocean where the water appears to be on fire called?

Answer: Bioluminescence

Giggly-5

1. Why was the computer always at the gym? It wanted to work on its software!

2. Why did the chemist go to the party? He wanted to test his social skills!

3. Why did the plant join the football team? It wanted to branch out!

4. Why did the calculator go to the park? It needed a break from all the number crunching!

5. Why did the scientist move to the city? He wanted to experiment with urban life!

Riddly-5: The Spectacular Light Display in the Sky

Clue	Problem
1.	I am a natural light display that occurs in the polar regions.
2.	I am caused by the interaction between charged particles from the Sun and the Earth's atmosphere.
3.	I come in a variety of colors, including green, pink, and purple.
4.	I am best observed in dark, clear skies away from light pollution.
5.	What is this natural light display that occurs in the polar regions called?

Answer: Aurora

Giggly-5

1. Why was the computer the best musician? It never missed a beat!

2. Why did the chemist go to the casino? He knew all the elements of gambling!

3. Why did the tree become a teacher? It had lots of growth potential!

4. Why did the math problem go to the psychologist? It needed help solving its issues!

5. Why did the scientist go to the farm? He wanted to study organic reactions!

Riddly-5: The Earth's Life-Sustaining Shield

Clue	Problem
1.	I am a protective layer surrounding the Earth.
2.	I help block harmful ultraviolet (UV) radiation from the Sun.
3.	I am composed of three atoms of oxygen bonded together.
4.	I can be found in both the stratosphere and the troposphere.
5.	What is the name of this protective layer that shields the Earth from UV radiation?

Answer: Ozone Layer

Giggly-5

1. Why did the computer get a job at the bank? It was great at data processing!

2. Why was the chemist so good at making coffee? He mastered the perfect solution!

3. Why did the plant become an actor? It was great at photosynthesizing emotions!

4. Why did the algebra book go on a diet? It wanted to reduce its problems!

5. Why did the scientist become a bartender? He wanted to mix things up!

Riddly-5: The Building Blocks of Matter

Clue	Problem
1.	We are the smallest particles that make up all matter.
2.	We are composed of protons, neutrons, and electrons.
3.	We cannot be broken down into simpler substances by chemical means.
4.	We come in different types, each with its own unique properties.
5.	What are these smallest particles that make up all matter called?

Answer: Atoms

Giggly-5

1. Why was the computer a great photographer? It had a good lens on life!

2. Why did the chemist open a restaurant? He knew all the elements of good food!

3. Why did the tree win the lottery? It was good at picking numbers!

4. Why was the math equation always tired? It was always working out problems!

5. Why did the scientist become a comedian? He wanted to experiment with humor!

Riddly-5: The Earth's Fiery Core

Clue	Problem
1.	I am the innermost layer of the Earth.
2.	I am primarily composed of iron and nickel.
3.	I am extremely hot, reaching temperatures up to 5700 degrees Celsius (10,000 degrees Fahrenheit).
4.	I generate the Earth's magnetic field.
5.	What is the name of this fiery layer at the center of the Earth?

Answer: Core

Giggly-5

1. Why did the computer go on vacation? It needed to reboot!

2. Why did the chemist become a DJ? He knew how to mix things up!

3. Why did the plant become a detective? It was great at getting to the root of problems!

4. Why was the calculator the best chef? It knew how to multiply ingredients!

5. Why did the scientist go to the bakery? He wanted to experiment with dough!

Riddly-5: The Cosmic Timekeepers

Clue	Problem
1.	We are astronomical objects that emit regular pulses of radiation.
2.	We are formed from the remnants of massive stars.
3.	Our pulsation rates are incredibly precise, making us reliable timekeepers.
4.	We are used by scientists to study the properties of matter under extreme conditions.
5.	What are these astronomical objects that emit regular pulses of radiation called?

Answer: Pulsars

Giggly-5

1. Why was the computer always confident? It had all the right software!

2. Why did the chemist become a gardener? He had a great reaction to plants!

3. Why did the tree become a philosopher? It was great at branching out ideas!

4. Why did the math book go to the beach? It needed to work on its tan lines!

5. Why did the scientist become a movie director? He wanted to experiment with different scenes!

Riddly-5: The Enigmatic Force of the Universe

Clue	Problem
1.	I am a mysterious force that is thought to be responsible for the accelerating expansion of the universe.
2.	My existence was first proposed to explain the discrepancy between the observed and predicted rates of expansion.
3.	I am named after a famous physicist who played a significant role in the development of modern physics.
4.	My nature and properties are still not fully understood by scientists.
5.	What is this enigmatic force thought to be responsible for the accelerating expansion of the universe?

Answer: Dark Energy

Giggly-5

1. Why did the computer join the army? It was great at following commands!

2. Why did the chemist become a stylist? He knew all about chemical reactions to hair dye!

3. Why did the plant become a psychologist? It was great at reading the room's environment!

4. Why did the calculator join the cooking class? It wanted to add some flavor to its life!

5. Why did the scientist go to the art museum? He wanted to study the science behind colors!

Riddly-5: The Ocean's Underwater Forests

Clue	Problem
1.	We are large, brown algae that form underwater forests in the ocean.
2.	We provide habitat and food for a wide variety of marine organisms.
3.	We are known for our kelp forests found in colder waters.
4.	We are primary producers and play a crucial role in the marine ecosystem.
5.	What are these large, brown algae that form underwater forests in the ocean called?

Answer: Kelp

Giggly-5

1. Why did the computer go to school? It wanted to boost its processing skills!

2. Why was the chemist always the life of the party? He had all the right reactions!

3. Why did the tree start a business? It believed in organic growth!

4. Why did the algebra book go to the doctor? It had too many problems!

5. Why did the scientist join the orchestra? He wanted to study the science of sound!

Riddly-5: The Human Body's Internal Communication System

Clue	Problem
1.	I am a complex network of organs and tissues that enables communication within the human body.
2.	I include structures such as the brain, spinal cord, and nerves.
3.	I transmit signals through electrical impulses and chemical messengers.
4.	I regulate bodily functions and allow for coordinated responses to stimuli.
5.	What is this complex network of organs and tissues that enables communication within the human body called?

Answer: Nervous System

Giggly-5

1. Why was the computer always calm? It knew how to keep its cool under pressure!

2. Why did the chemist go to the music festival? He was studying the chemistry of sound!

3. Why did the plant join the gym? It wanted to grow stronger!

4. Why did the calculator join the debate team? It knew how to argue with logic!

5. Why did the scientist go to the dance club? He wanted to study the physics of motion!

Riddly-5: The Elusive Subatomic Particle

Clue	Problem
1.	I am an elementary particle that carries a negative electric charge.
2.	I am a fundamental building block of matter.
3.	I orbit around the nucleus of an atom.
4.	I am involved in chemical reactions and the flow of electricity.
5.	What is this elusive subatomic particle that carries a negative electric charge?

Answer: Electron

Giggly-5

1. Why did the computer go to the library? It needed to update its knowledge database!

2. Why did the chemist go to the cooking class? He wanted to mix the right ingredients!

3. Why did the tree go to the barber? It needed a trim!

4. Why did the math book join the book club? It wanted to add more stories to its life!

5. Why did the scientist go to the swimming pool? He wanted to study the fluid dynamics!

Riddly-5: The Earth's Luminous Neighbor

Clue	Problem
1.	I am the closest celestial body to Earth.
2.	I provide light and heat to the Earth.
3.	I am a medium-sized star located in the center of our solar system.
4.	I am made up of hot, glowing gases.
5.	What is the name of the Earth's luminous neighbor in the sky?

Answer: Sun

Giggly-5

1. Why did the computer go to the movie? It wanted to download some entertainment!

2. Why was the chemist always the best chef? He knew the formula for a perfect meal!

3. Why did the tree go to the comedy club? It wanted to branch out into humor!

4. Why did the calculator go to the spa? It needed a break from number crunching!

5. Why did the scientist join the basketball team? He wanted to study the physics of the game!

Riddly-5: The Messenger of the Stars

Clue	Problem
1.	I am a celestial body that orbits a star.
2.	I am composed of rock and/or ice.
3.	I can have a tail that becomes visible when I approach the Sun.
4.	I come in various sizes, from tiny dust particles to large objects.
5.	What is this celestial body that orbits a star and can have a visible tail called?

Answer: Comet

Giggly-5

1. Why did the computer go to the zoo? It wanted to scan some wild data!

2. Why did the chemist join the circus? He wanted to bring more reactions to his life!

3. Why did the plant go to the concert? It wanted to absorb the vibes!

4. Why did the math book go to the concert? It wanted to multiply its fun!

5. Why did the scientist go to the ice-skating rink? He wanted to study the physics of gliding!

Riddly-5: The Airborne Seed Travelers

Clue	Problem
1.	We are lightweight structures produced by plants for dispersal.
2.	We have unique adaptations that help us travel through the air.
3.	We can be carried by wind, water, or animals to new locations.
4.	We are essential for the reproduction and dispersal of many plant species.
5.	What are these lightweight structures produced by plants for dispersal called?

Answer: Seeds

Giggly-5

1. Why did the computer go to the beach? It wanted to surf the net in real life!

2. Why did the chemist go to the gym? He wanted to work on his reactions!

3. Why did the tree go to the fashion show? It wanted to spruce up its style!

4. Why did the calculator go to the music concert? It wanted to count the beats!

5. Why did the scientist go to the comedy show? He wanted to understand the chemistry of humor!

Riddly-5: The Silent Builders of Coral Reefs

Clue	Problem
1.	We are tiny, soft-bodied animals that build massive underwater structures.
2.	We form colonies and secrete calcium carbonate to create our protective exoskeletons.
3.	We are found in warm, shallow waters, often in tropical regions.
4.	We provide habitat and shelter for a wide variety of marine species.
5.	What are these tiny animals that build massive underwater structures called?

Answer: Corals

Giggly-5

1. Why did the computer join the circus? It loved to juggle data!

2. Why did the chemist become a baker? He had all the ingredients for success!

3. Why did the plant start a band? It had great roots in music!

4. Why did the math equation become a travel blogger? It loved to go off on tangents!

5. Why did the scientist start painting? He wanted to blend the colors of science!

Riddly-5: The Earth's Natural Satellite

Clue	Problem
1.	I am a celestial object that orbits around a planet.
2.	I reflect sunlight and appear bright in the night sky.
3.	I have a significant influence on Earth's tides.
4.	I am the only natural satellite of Earth.
5.	What is the name of the Earth's natural satellite?

Answer: Moon

Giggly-5

1. Why did the computer go to the museum? It wanted to enhance its historical database!

2. Why did the chemist start a band? He was all about creating good chemistry!

3. Why did the tree go to the music festival? It was pining for good tunes!

4. Why did the math book become a chef? It knew all about pie!

5. Why did the scientist start a gardening hobby? He wanted to explore botany!

Riddly-5: The Earth's Protective Shield

Clue	Problem
1.	I am a layer of charged particles surrounding the Earth.
2.	I am located in the upper atmosphere and protect the Earth from harmful solar wind.
3.	I am responsible for creating the beautiful aurora borealis and aurora australis.
4.	I can be affected by solar activity and can cause disruptions in radio communications.
5.	What is this layer of charged particles surrounding the Earth called?

Answer: Magnetosphere

Giggly-5

1. Why was the computer a great chess player? It could process all possible moves!

2. Why did the chemist start a comedy show? He loved causing reactions!

3. Why did the plant join the orchestra? It had a natural rhythm!

4. Why did the math problem go to therapy? It was feeling too complex!

5. Why did the scientist become a poet? He found beauty in the laws of nature!

Riddly-5: The Mighty Geological Shapers

Clue	Problem
1.	We are natural processes that shape the Earth's surface.
2.	We can occur due to tectonic activity, weathering, erosion, and deposition.
3.	We can create mountains, valleys, canyons, and other landforms.
4.	We are responsible for the continuous changes in the Earth's landscape.
5.	What are these natural processes that shape the Earth's surface called?

Answer: Geological Forces

Giggly-5

1. Why did the computer get a job at the airport? It was good at running flight simulations!

2. Why did the chemist become a chef? He loved experimenting with flavors!

3. Why did the tree start writing a book? It had a story to sprout!

4. Why did the math equation join the theater? It loved to solve dramas!

5. Why did the scientist start a rock band? He was intrigued by sound waves!

Riddly-5: The Guardians of Biodiversity

Clue	Problem
1.	We are areas of land or water that are protected to conserve biodiversity.
2.	We provide habitat for a wide variety of plant and animal species.
3.	We help preserve endangered and threatened species.
4.	We promote sustainable use of natural resources and environmental education.
5.	What are these areas of land or water that are protected to conserve biodiversity called?

Answer: Protected Areas

Giggly-5

1. Why did the computer go to the casino? It calculated the odds in its favor!

2. Why did the chemist become a storyteller? He loved mixing elements of surprise!

3. Why did the tree go on a date? It wanted to branch out socially!

4. Why did the calculator join the choir? It knew the numbers of a good tune!

5. Why did the scientist become a dancer? He wanted to understand the physics of movement!

Riddly-5: The Green Lungs of the Earth

Clue	Problem
1.	We are extensive areas covered with trees and vegetation.
2.	We play a crucial role in producing oxygen and absorbing carbon dioxide.
3.	We provide habitat for numerous plant and animal species.
4.	We help regulate the Earth's climate and maintain the water cycle.
5.	What are these extensive areas covered with trees and vegetation called?

Answer: Forests

Giggly-5

1. Why did the computer become a detective? It was good at decoding mysteries!
2. Why did the chemist start a brewery? He was interested in the chemistry of beer!
3. Why did the plant join the debate team? It was good at turning over a new leaf!
4. Why did the math book join the orchestra? It wanted to play with numbers in a new way!
5. Why did the scientist start a cooking class? He was interested in the science of gastronomy!

Riddly-5: The Mysterious Energy of the Universe

Clue	Problem
1.	I am a form of energy that permeates the entire universe.
2.	I have no mass or charge, but I can influence the behavior of matter and space.
3.	I am responsible for the accelerated expansion of the universe.
4.	My existence was confirmed through astronomical observations.
5.	What is this mysterious form of energy that permeates the entire universe called?

Answer: Dark Energy

Giggly-5

1. Why did the computer join a book club? It wanted to expand its memory!

2. Why did the chemist start a travel blog? He was interested in the elements of different cultures!

3. Why did the tree go to the fair? It wanted to enjoy the bark-carnival!

4. Why did the math equation join a rock band? It wanted to go off on a tangent!

5. Why did the scientist join a magic show? He wanted to unravel the science behind illusions!

Riddly-5: The Flying Architects

Clue	Problem
1.	We are social insects known for our complex colonies and organized societies.
2.	We build intricate nests or hives using materials like mud, wax, or wood.
3.	We have specialized castes, including workers, drones, and a queen.
4.	We play a vital role in pollination and ecosystem balance.
5.	What are these social insects known for their complex colonies and organized societies called?

Answer: Bees

Giggly-5

1. Why did the computer go to the music festival? It wanted to download new tunes!

2. Why did the chemist start a restaurant? He knew how to combine the right elements!

3. Why did the plant join a dance group? It wanted to sway to the rhythm!

4. Why did the math book join a gardening club? It wanted to grow its knowledge!

5. Why did the scientist start a fashion line? He was intrigued by the physics of fabrics!

Riddly-5: The Rainbows of the Night Sky

Clue	Problem
1.	I am a natural phenomenon that occurs when light interacts with water droplets in the atmosphere.
2.	I appear as a circular arc of colors in the sky.
3.	I am caused by the reflection, refraction, and dispersion of light.
4.	I am often seen after rainfall or when moisture is present in the air.
5.	What is this natural phenomenon that appears as a circular arc of colors in the sky called?

Answer: Rainbow

Giggly-5

1. Why did the computer join the photography club? It was great at processing images!

2. Why did the chemist start a coffee shop? He loved brewing up reactions!

3. Why did the tree become a motivational speaker? It always stood tall and firm!

4. Why did the equation join the football team? It loved the idea of dividing the field!

5. Why did the scientist become a songwriter? He believed in the chemistry of melodies!

Riddly-5: The Fiery Performers in the Sky

Clue	Problem
1.	We are natural atmospheric phenomena that occur during thunderstorms.
2.	We are characterized by bright, branching discharges of electricity.
3.	We can reach temperatures hotter than the surface of the Sun.
4.	We produce a loud cracking or rumbling sound called thunder.
5.	What are these natural atmospheric phenomena that occur during thunderstorms called?

Answer: Lightning

Giggly-5

1. Why did the computer become a traffic cop? It was great at processing signals!

2. Why did the chemist become a gourmet chef? He wanted to experiment with molecular gastronomy!

3. Why did the plant join a book club? It wanted to grow its literary roots!

4. Why did the math book start a vlog? It loved the idea of 'summing up' experiences!

5. Why did the scientist become a yoga teacher? He was interested in the physics of postures!

Riddly-5: The Mysterious Force That Shapes the Universe

Clue	Problem
1.	I am a fundamental force that governs the interactions between particles in the universe.
2.	I am responsible for holding atoms and molecules together.
3.	I am the force behind chemical reactions and the formation of compounds.
4.	I can be attractive or repulsive, depending on the charges of the particles involved.
5.	What is this fundamental force that governs the interactions between particles called?

Answer: Electromagnetic Force

Giggly-5

1. Why did the computer become a traffic analyst? It had the capacity to process real-time data!

2. Why did the chemist become a wine maker? He understood the science behind fermentation!

3. Why did the tree start a publishing house? It wanted to turn new leaves into books!

4. Why did the math book become a basketball coach? It understood the angle of the shot!

5. Why did the scientist become a food critic? He loved the science behind taste!

Riddly-5: The Towering Giants of the Forest

Clue	Problem
1.	We are the tallest living organisms on Earth.
2.	We are woody plants that have a significant impact on the environment.
3.	We can live for hundreds or even thousands of years.
4.	We produce oxygen, provide habitat, and store carbon dioxide.
5.	What are these tall, woody plants that have a significant impact on the environment called?

Answer: Trees

Giggly-5

1. Why did the computer become a chess master? It could calculate all possible moves!

2. Why did the chemist become a firework manufacturer? He knew the elements for vibrant colors!

3. Why did the tree become a philosophy professor? It believed in deep rooted thoughts!

4. Why did the math book become a fitness trainer? It knew the formula for burning calories!

5. Why did the scientist become a music conductor? He was fascinated by the physics of sound!

Riddly-5: The Earth's Natural Air Conditioning System

Clue	Problem
1.	I am a natural process that cools down the Earth's surface and lower atmosphere.
2.	I occur when water evaporates from bodies of water and transpires from plants.
3.	I release latent heat, cooling the surrounding air.
4.	I help regulate temperature and create a more comfortable environment.
5.	What is this natural process that cools down the Earth's surface and lower atmosphere called?

Answer: Evaporation

Giggly-5

1. Why did the computer start a home decor business? It loved designing algorithms!

2. Why did the chemist become a DJ? He was good at mixing beats!

3. Why did the tree start a blog? It wanted to share its natural beauty!

4. Why did the math book start a travel agency? It loved calculating adventures!

5. Why did the scientist become a filmmaker? He was interested in the science behind storytelling!

Riddly-5: The Secretive Powerhouses of Cells

Clue	Problem
1.	We are the energy-producing organelles found in cells.
2.	We are often referred to as the "powerhouses" of the cell.
3.	We generate energy in the form of ATP through cellular respiration.
4.	We have our own DNA and reproduce independently within the cell.
5.	What are these energy-producing organelles found in cells called?

Answer: Mitochondria

Giggly-5

1. Why did the computer become a personal trainer? It could calculate the best workout routine!

2. Why did the chemist become a comedian? He loved a good chemical reaction!

3. Why did the tree become a life coach? It believed in personal growth!

4. Why did the equation join the drama club? It loved to be the center of a plot!

5. Why did the scientist become a perfume maker? He was intrigued by the chemistry of scents!

Riddly-5: The Mighty Ecosystem Engineers

Clue	Problem
1.	We are organisms that significantly alter our environment to create habitats for ourselves and other species.
2.	We build structures like dams, burrows, or nests.
3.	We can change water flow, nutrient distribution, and landscape features.
4.	We have a profound impact on biodiversity and ecosystem dynamics.
5.	What are these organisms that significantly alter their environment called?

Answer: Ecosystem Engineers

Giggly-5

1. Why did the computer join the army? It was good at breaking codes!

2. Why did the chemist become a sculptor? He loved moulding elements!

3. Why did the tree join a soccer team? It was always branching out!

4. Why did the math book become a fortune teller? It knew how to predict patterns!

5. Why did the scientist become a pastry chef? He was interested in the science behind baking!

Riddly-5: The Silent Guardians of the Night

Clue	Problem
1.	We are nocturnal flying mammals.
2.	We have wings and can navigate in complete darkness.
3.	We are known for our exceptional hearing and echolocation abilities.
4.	We play important roles in pollination, seed dispersal, and pest control.
5.	What are these nocturnal flying mammals with exceptional hearing and echolocation abilities called?

Answer: Bats

Giggly-5

1. Why did the computer become a meteorologist? It was great at forecasting patterns!

2. Why did the chemist start a cosmetics line? He understood the chemistry of beauty!

3. Why did the tree join a jazz band? It had a great rhythm!

4. Why did the equation become a real estate agent? It loved to solve space issues!

5. Why did the scientist become a dance instructor? He wanted to study the dynamics of movement!

Riddly-5: The Invisible Building Blocks of Matter

Clue	Problem
1.	We are subatomic particles that make up protons and neutrons.
2.	We have no electric charge.
3.	We are held together by strong nuclear forces.
4.	We are called "quarks" and come in different types: up and down.
5.	What are these invisible particles that make up protons and neutrons called?

Answer: Quarks

Giggly-5

1. Why did the computer join the fashion industry? It was an expert at weaving codes!

2. Why did the chemist become a jeweler? He was good at combining precious elements!

3. Why did the tree start a clothing brand? It loved organic fibers!

4. Why did the math book become a meteorologist? It knew how to calculate the probability of rain!

5. Why did the scientist become a gardener? He wanted to study the biology of plants!

Riddly-5: The Glowing Nighttime Creatures

Clue	Problem
1.	We are small, bioluminescent organisms that light up the night.
2.	We are found in various marine and terrestrial habitats.
3.	We produce our own light through a chemical reaction.
4.	We use our bioluminescence for communication, attraction, or defense.
5.	What are these small, bioluminescent organisms that light up the night called?

Answer: Fireflies

Giggly-5

1. Why did the computer become a magician? It was an expert at binary tricks!

2. Why did the chemist become a brewmaster? He was familiar with all the right elements for a good brew!

3. Why did the tree become a poet? It had deep roots in emotions!

4. Why did the math book join a rock band? It loved to count beats!

5. Why did the scientist become a landscape artist? He wanted to capture the chemistry of colors!

Riddly-5: The Ocean's Silent Giants

Clue	Problem
1.	We are the largest animals on Earth.
2.	We are marine mammals that feed on tiny shrimp-like animals called krill.
3.	We undertake long migrations, singing complex songs along the way.
4.	We play an important role in the ocean ecosystem and carbon cycle.
5.	What are these largest animals on Earth, marine mammals that feed on krill called?

Answer: Whales

Giggly-5

1. Why did the computer start a music streaming platform? It had great algorithms for playlists!

2. Why did the chemist become a chocolatier? He knew the formula for the perfect sweetness!

3. Why did the tree become an architect? It understood the importance of good roots!

4. Why did the math book become a detective? It knew how to solve mysteries!

5. Why did the scientist become a tour guide? He wanted to explain the geology of landscapes!

Riddly-5: The Builders of Intricate Homes

Clue	Problem
1.	We are social insects that construct complex structures for our colonies.
2.	We build intricate homes using a combination of mud, saliva, and other materials.
3.	We play important roles in pollination and ecosystem balance.
4.	We are known for our ability to regulate temperature within our nests.
5.	What are these social insects that build intricate homes called?

Answer: Termites

Giggly-5

1. Why did the computer become a travel agent? It loved to compute the best routes!
2. Why did the chemist become a hair stylist? He understood the reaction between color and hair!
3. Why did the plant become a life coach? It believed in growth and blooming!
4. Why did the math book become a rapper? It was all about spitting numbers!
5. Why did the scientist become a dance teacher? He mastered the physics of movement!

Riddly-5: The Silent Stalkers of the Night

Clue	Problem
1.	We are nocturnal birds of prey.
2.	We are known for our silent flight and exceptional vision.
3.	We have sharp talons and beaks for catching and tearing our prey.
4.	We play an important role in controlling rodent populations.
5.	What are these nocturnal birds of prey with silent flight called?

Answer: Owls

Giggly-5

1. Why did the computer become a chef? It loved to byte into good food!
2. Why did the chemist become a sculptor? He loved molding elements!
3. Why did the plant become a DJ? It loved to drop the beets!
4. Why did the math book become a historian? It understood the numbers behind history!
5. Why did the scientist become a surfer? He loved the science of waves!

Riddly-5: The Dynamic Forces Within the Earth

Clue	Problem
1.	We are responsible for shaping the Earth's surface.
2.	We occur due to the movement of tectonic plates.
3.	We can cause earthquakes, volcanic eruptions, and the formation of mountains.
4.	We are a result of the heat and convection currents in the Earth's interior.
5.	What are these dynamic forces within the Earth called?

Answer: Plate Tectonics

Giggly-5

1. Why did the computer become a baker? It was great at measuring ingredients!

2. Why did the chemist become a florist? He knew how to preserve flowers!

3. Why did the tree start a record label? It believed in growing talent!

4. Why did the math book become a chef? It knew the perfect formula for tasty dishes!

5. Why did the scientist become a zookeeper? He was passionate about animal behavior!

Riddly-5: The Guardians of the Coral Reefs

Clue	Problem
1.	We are colorful marine fish found in coral reef ecosystems.
2.	We form symbiotic relationships with anemones for protection.
3.	We are known for our vibrant colors and unique patterns.
4.	We play important roles in maintaining the health and biodiversity of coral reefs.
5.	What are these colorful marine fish found in coral reef ecosystems called?

Answer: Clownfish

Giggly-5

1. Why did the computer become a city planner? It was great at optimizing paths!

2. Why did the chemist become a perfume maker? He had the perfect formula for pleasant smells!

3. Why did the tree become a furniture designer? It knew all about the strength of wood!

4. Why did the math book become a historian? It was interested in calculating dates!

5. Why did the scientist become a park ranger? He wanted to study ecosystems up close!

Riddly-5: The Masters of Flight

Clue	Problem
1.	We are warm-blooded vertebrates with the ability to fly.
2.	We have feathered wings and hollow bones.
3.	We are the only group of animals capable of sustained powered flight.
4.	We come in various shapes and sizes, from small hummingbirds to large eagles.
5.	What are these warm-blooded vertebrates with the ability to fly called?

Answer: Birds

Giggly-5

1. Why did the computer become a tailor? It knew all about threading processes!
2. Why did the chemist become a fitness coach? He understood the chemistry of exercise!
3. Why did the plant become a guidance counselor? It loved helping others grow!
4. Why did the math book become a relationship coach? It was great at solving problems!
5. Why did the scientist become a landscape artist? He loved the science of colors!

Riddly-5: The Earth's Natural Satellites

Clue	Problem
1.	We are objects that orbit around planets or dwarf planets.
2.	We are smaller than moons and have irregular shapes.
3.	We are remnants from the early formation of the solar system.
4.	We can be found in asteroid belts or the outer regions of the solar system.
5.	What are these objects that orbit around planets or dwarf planets called?

Answer: Asteroids

Giggly-5

1. Why did the computer become a philosopher? It was great at processing thoughts!

2. Why did the chemist become a beauty blogger? She knew all about the chemistry of cosmetics!

3. Why did the plant become a philosopher? It knew the roots of deep thoughts!

4. Why did the math book become a songwriter? It knew how to count beats!

5. Why did the scientist become a wine maker? He understood the chemistry of a good vintage!

Riddly-5: The Mysterious Properties of Light

Clue	Problem
1.	I am a form of electromagnetic radiation.
2.	I can behave both as a particle and a wave.
3.	I travel at a speed of approximately 299,792 kilometers per second.
4.	I am essential for vision and provide information about the world around us.
5.	What is this form of electromagnetic radiation that behaves as both a particle and a wave called?

Answer: Light

Giggly-5

1. Why did the computer become a fortune teller? It had predictive algorithms!
2. Why did the chemist become a bartender? He had the solution to everything!
3. Why did the plant become a food critic? It had a fresh palate!
4. Why did the math book become a motivational speaker? It knew that the possibilities are infinite!
5. Why did the scientist become a DJ? He loved the physics of sound!

Riddly-5: The Invisible Boundary in Space

Clue	Problem
1.	I am a region of space beyond the Earth's atmosphere.
2.	I contain a high concentration of charged particles.
3.	I can cause disruptions in satellite communications and auroras.
4.	I am influenced by solar activity and the Earth's magnetic field.
5.	What is this region of space beyond the Earth's atmosphere called?

Answer: Magnetosphere

Giggly-5

1. Why did the computer become a fashion designer? It had a byte for style!
2. Why did the chemist become a pastry chef? He loved a good chemical reaction!
3. Why did the plant become a weather forecaster? It was great at predicting spring showers!
4. Why did the math book become a stand-up comedian? It knew that timing is everything!
5. Why did the scientist become an event planner? He knew the formula for a great party!

Riddly-5: The Living Rainbows

Clue	Problem
1.	We are diverse ecosystems with a high concentration of organisms.
2.	We are found in freshwater or marine environments.
3.	We provide food, shelter, and breeding grounds for numerous species.
4.	We are highly productive and contribute to the overall health of the planet.
5.	What are these diverse ecosystems with a high concentration of organisms called?

Answer: Coral Reefs

Giggly-5

1. Why did the computer become an astronaut? It was good at calculating trajectories!

2. Why did the chemist become a soap maker? He had the formula for bubbly solutions!

3. Why did the tree become a motivational speaker? It stood for growth and resilience!

4. Why did the math book become a financial adviser? It knew all about increasing interest!

5. Why did the scientist become a nature photographer? He wanted to capture the chemistry of life!

Riddly-5: The Earth's Mighty Giants

Clue	Problem
1.	We are the tallest land animals on Earth.
2.	We have long necks and legs, allowing us to reach high vegetation.
3.	We are known for our distinctive patterns of spots or patches.
4.	We are herbivores, feeding primarily on leaves and twigs.
5.	What are these tall land animals with long necks and distinctive patterns called?

Answer: Giraffes

Giggly-5

1. Why did the computer become a weather forecaster? It was skilled at predicting patterns!

2. Why did the chemist become a baker? He knew the right reaction for a perfect rise!

3. Why did the tree become a yoga instructor? It knew the importance of grounding!

4. Why did the math book become a dating advisor? It knew the probability of a perfect match!

5. Why did the scientist become a hairstylist? He was interested in the biology of hair!

Riddly-5: The Marvels of Underwater Architecture

Clue	Problem
1.	We are tiny marine invertebrates that construct intricate structures.
2.	We use calcium carbonate to build our protective exoskeletons.
3.	We form extensive colonies, creating diverse habitats for other organisms.
4.	We are found in oceans around the world, from shallow waters to deep-sea environments.
5.	What are these tiny marine invertebrates that construct intricate structures called?

Answer: Coral Polyps

Giggly-5

1. Why did the computer join a band? It heard they needed more processing power!

2. Why did the chemist start making candles? He had a flare for reactions!

3. Why did the tree become a life coach? It believed in personal growth!

4. Why did the math book start a travel agency? It loved calculating distances!

5. Why did the scientist start a cooking show? He wanted to mix chemistry with cuisine!

Riddly-5: The Silent Navigators of the Sky

Clue	Problem
1.	We are migratory birds known for our incredible navigation skills.
2.	We can travel thousands of kilometers during our annual migrations.
3.	We use celestial cues, Earth's magnetic field, and visual landmarks to find our way.
4.	We undertake these long journeys to find food, breeding grounds, or favorable climates.
5.	What are these migratory birds known for their incredible navigation skills called?

Answer: Migratory Birds

Giggly-5

1. Why did the computer start a matchmaking service? It excelled in binary compatibility!

2. Why did the chemist open a laundry service? He had a solution for every stain!

3. Why did the tree become a fashion designer? It was a natural at making patterns!

4. Why did the math book become a real estate agent? It knew all about square footage!

5. Why did the scientist become a dance instructor? He understood the physics of movement!

Riddly-5: The Earth's Powerful Forces of Change

Clue	Problem
1.	We are natural processes that constantly shape the Earth's surface.
2.	We can cause the formation of mountains, valleys, and other landforms.
3.	We occur due to tectonic activity, erosion, and deposition.
4.	We can be gradual or sudden, with the potential for significant impacts.
5.	What are these natural processes that constantly shape the Earth's surface called?

Answer: Geologic Forces

Giggly-5

1. Why did the computer become a sports commentator? It had unmatched processing speed!

2. Why did the chemist become a make-up artist? He knew the compounds for beauty!

3. Why did the tree start a music label? It knew how to branch out talent!

4. Why did the math book become a fortune teller? It believed in the power of numbers!

5. Why did the scientist become a theatre director? He was passionate about the biology of emotions!

Riddly-5: The Invisible Shield in the Sky

Clue	Problem
1.	I am a layer of gases that surrounds the Earth.
2.	I protect the Earth from harmful ultraviolet radiation.
3.	I help regulate the Earth's temperature by trapping heat from the Sun.
4.	I contain a thin layer called the ozone layer.
5.	What is this layer of gases that protects the Earth called?

Answer: Atmosphere

Giggly-5

1. Why did the computer become a race car driver? It loved processing speed!

2. Why did the chemist start a cleaning business? He knew all about getting reactions out of dirt!

3. Why did the tree become a mindfulness coach? It was in touch with its roots!

4. Why did the math book start a delivery service? It could calculate the fastest route!

5. Why did the scientist become a bartender? He had the right mix for every solution!

Riddly-5: The Mysteries of the Microscopic World

Clue	Problem
1.	We are tiny organisms that cannot be seen with the naked eye.
2.	We exist in various forms such as bacteria, viruses, or fungi.
3.	We play crucial roles in ecosystem processes and can have both positive and negative impacts.
4.	We can cause diseases or provide essential services like decomposition.
5.	What are these tiny organisms that cannot be seen with the naked eye called?

Answer: Microorganisms

Giggly-5

1. Why did the computer become an archaeologist? It loved digging up data!

2. Why did the chemist start a tattoo studio? He had the inkling for permanent solutions!

3. Why did the tree become an interior decorator? It had a knack for natural beauty!

4. Why did the math book start a gym? It knew all about the numbers in fitness!

5. Why did the scientist become a film director? He wanted to showcase the science behind storytelling!

Riddly-5: The Invisible Dance of Atoms

Clue	Problem
1.	We are the basic units of matter.
2.	We consist of a nucleus surrounded by electrons.
3.	We can combine to form molecules through chemical bonds.
4.	We are constantly in motion, vibrating and colliding with one another.
5.	What are these basic units of matter called?

Answer: Atoms

Giggly-5

1. Why did the computer become a novelist? It was fantastic at processing words!

2. Why did the chemist open a brewery? He knew all about mixing elements for a perfect brew!

3. Why did the tree start a landscaping business? It had a natural understanding of growth patterns!

4. Why did the math book become a meteorologist? It knew how to calculate the odds of rain!

5. Why did the scientist start a beauty salon? He understood the biology of skin!

Riddly-5: The Guardians of Freshwater Ecosystems

Clue	Problem
1.	We are diverse ecosystems found in bodies of freshwater.
2.	We provide habitat for numerous plant and animal species.
3.	We play vital roles in water filtration, nutrient cycling, and flood regulation.
4.	We are threatened by pollution, habitat loss, and invasive species.
5.	What are these diverse ecosystems found in bodies of freshwater called?

Answer: Wetlands

Giggly-5

1. Why did the computer become a movie critic? It had a good processor for plot analysis!

2. Why did the chemist become a coffee barista? He had the perfect formula for a great cup of joe!

3. Why did the tree start a wellness clinic? It knew the value of grounding!

4. Why did the math book start a job consultancy? It knew how to add value to a career!

5. Why did the scientist become a fitness trainer? He understood the physics of body movement!

Riddly-5: The Secret Codes of Life

Clue	Problem
1.	We are long molecules that contain the instructions for life.
2.	We consist of a sequence of nucleotides.
3.	We determine an organism's traits and characteristics.
4.	We are passed from parents to offspring during reproduction.
5.	What are these long molecules that contain the instructions for life called?

Answer: DNA (Deoxyribonucleic Acid)

Giggly-5

1. Why did the computer become a detective? It was excellent at decoding patterns!

2. Why did the chemist start a restaurant? He knew the right ingredients for a fantastic reaction!

3. Why did the tree start an art school? It believed in cultivating creativity!

4. Why did the math book become a magician? It knew the formula for illusions!

5. Why did the scientist become a marine biologist? He was interested in the chemistry of the ocean!

Riddly-5: The Guardians of the Rainforest

Clue	Problem
1.	We are diverse ecosystems characterized by dense vegetation and high rainfall.
2.	We are home to a wide variety of plant and animal species.
3.	We play a crucial role in maintaining the Earth's climate and oxygen production.
4.	We are rapidly disappearing due to deforestation and human activities.
5.	What are these diverse ecosystems characterized by dense vegetation and high rainfall called?

Answer: Rainforests

Giggly-5

1. Why did the computer start a robotics company? It knew all about automation!

2. Why did the chemist start a cosmetics company? He had the formula for beauty!

3. Why did the tree become a psychologist? It understood the importance of deep roots!

4. Why did the math book become a pilot? It loved calculating flight paths!

5. Why did the scientist become a wedding planner? He knew all about chemistry between people!

Riddly-5: The Dancing Lights in the Polar Skies

Clue	Problem
1.	We are natural light displays that occur in the polar regions.
2.	We are caused by interactions between the Earth's magnetic field and solar particles.
3.	We appear as colorful, shifting curtains or bands of light in the sky.
4.	We are most commonly seen near the Earth's magnetic poles.
5.	What are these natural light displays that occur in the polar regions called?

Answer: Aurora

Giggly-5

1. Why did the computer start a fashion label? It knew all about the design matrix!

2. Why did the chemist become a chocolatier? He had a sweet tooth for reactions!

3. Why did the tree become a sculptor? It loved carving out details!

4. Why did the math book become a tailor? It knew all about measurements!

5. Why did the scientist become a skydiving instructor? He loved the physics of free fall!

Riddly-5: The Earth's Natural Recyclers

Clue	Problem
1.	We are organisms that break down dead organic matter.
2.	We play a vital role in nutrient cycling and soil formation.
3.	We come in various forms, such as bacteria, fungi, and worms.
4.	We convert organic waste into simpler compounds that can be reused by other organisms.
5.	What are these organisms that break down dead organic matter called?

Answer: Decomposers

Giggly-5

1. Why did the computer become a librarian? It had a database of knowledge!

2. Why did the chemist start a bakery? He knew all about the reactions for a perfect loaf!

3. Why did the tree become an architect? It knew about structural strength!

4. Why did the math book become a chess coach? It knew all the right moves!

5. Why did the scientist become a tour guide? He loved explaining the science of landmarks!

Riddly-5: The Lifeblood of the Earth

Clue	Problem
1.	We are essential for all forms of life on Earth.
2.	We cover approximately 71% of the Earth's surface.
3.	We regulate temperature, support biodiversity, and influence weather patterns.
4.	We exist in various forms, including oceans, seas, lakes, and rivers.
5.	What is this essential resource that covers a significant portion of the Earth's surface called?

Answer: Water

Giggly-5

1. Why did the computer become a DJ? It had a hard drive for beats!

2. Why did the chemist become a gardener? He knew the formula for perfect soil!

3. Why did the tree become a sommelier? It had a natural sense of tannins!

4. Why did the math book become a baseball coach? It knew all the angles!

5. Why did the scientist become a sommelier? He understood the chemistry of wine!

Riddly-5: The Guardians of the Savanna

Clue	Problem
1.	We are vast grassland ecosystems with scattered trees and shrubs.
2.	We are home to a diverse range of herbivores, carnivores, and migratory birds.
3.	We are characterized by a distinct wet and dry season.
4.	We are threatened by habitat loss and climate change.
5.	What are these vast grassland ecosystems with scattered trees and shrubs called?

Answer: Savannas

Giggly-5

1. Why did the computer start an online dating service? It knew all about making connections!

2. Why did the chemist start a candle making business? He had the perfect formula for a slow burn!

3. Why did the tree become a yoga instructor? It knew how to stay grounded!

4. Why did the math book start an investment firm? It knew all about growing numbers!

5. Why did the scientist become a chef? He loved the science behind a great dish!

Riddly-5: The Builders of Aquatic Fortresses

Clue	Problem
1.	We are tiny marine invertebrates that construct intricate structures.
2.	We build our homes using calcium carbonate and other materials.
3.	We form extensive colonies that provide habitat and protection for various organisms.
4.	We are found in oceans around the world, creating diverse and vibrant ecosystems.
5.	What are these tiny marine invertebrates that construct intricate structures called?

Answer: Coral Polyps

Giggly-5

1. Why don't scientists trust atoms? Because they make up everything!
2. Why was the physics book full of self-esteem? Because it had all the "matter"!
3. What do you call a biologist who can play the piano? A musical gene-ius!
4. What did one tectonic plate say to the other when they bumped into each other? Sorry, my fault!
5. Why don't chemists like nitrates? They're cheaper than day rates!

Riddly-5: The Mesmerizing Patterns of the Snowflakes

Clue	Problem
1.	We are unique ice crystals that form in the Earth's atmosphere.
2.	We have intricate and symmetrical patterns.
3.	We are formed through the process of crystallization.
4.	We are delicate and beautiful, with no two snowflakes being exactly the same.
5.	What are these unique ice crystals that form intricate and symmetrical patterns called?

Answer: Snowflakes

Giggly-5

1. Why did the scientist go to the tanning salon? Because he wanted to get a bronze reaction!

2. What did the thermometer say to the graduated cylinder? "You may have graduated but I've got many degrees!"

3. What did the biologist wear on his first date? Designer genes!

4. Why did the atom split? It wanted to be open-minded!

5. Why did the computer take its hat off? Because it was CAPS LOCK!

Riddly-5: The Masters of Camouflage

Clue	Problem
1.	We are animals that can change our skin color or patterns to blend with the surroundings.
2.	We use camouflage for hunting, avoiding predators, or attracting mates.
3.	We have specialized skin cells or structures that allow us to change our appearance.
4.	We can match the colors and textures of our environment almost perfectly.
5.	What are these animals that can change their skin color or patterns to blend with the surroundings called?

Answer: Masters of Camouflage

Giggly-5

1. Why did the computer become a landscaper? It loved bits of nature!
2. Why did the chemist become a coffee roaster? He knew the formula for the perfect brew!
3. Why did the plant start a travel agency? It wanted to branch out!
4. Why did the math book become a magician? It knew all the angles for the perfect trick!
5. Why did the scientist become a comedian? He knew the formula for laughter!

Riddly-5: The Guardians of the Sky

Clue	Problem
1.	We are large birds of prey known for our powerful beaks and sharp talons.
2.	We have exceptional eyesight and keen hunting skills.
3.	We play important roles in maintaining the balance of ecosystems by controlling rodent populations.
4.	We build large nests called eyries on high perches or cliffs.
5.	What are these large birds of prey known for their powerful beaks and sharp talons called?

Answer: Guardians of the Sky

Giggly-5

1. Why did the computer become a mystery novelist? It loved encoding suspense!
2. Why did the chemist become a cheese maker? He had a good culture!
3. Why did the plant become a baker? It knew all about the perfect dough rising!
4. Why did the math book become a detective? It was great at adding up clues!
5. Why did the scientist become a life coach? He understood the science of happiness!

Riddly-5: The Guardians of the Forest Floor

Clue	Problem
1.	We are small, often overlooked creatures that play vital roles in the forest ecosystem.
2.	We break down organic matter, improving soil fertility.
3.	We form mutualistic relationships with plants, aiding in nutrient absorption.
4.	We are highly diverse and can be found in various habitats worldwide.
5.	What are these small creatures that play vital roles in the forest ecosystem called?

Answer: Guardians of the Forest Floor

Giggly-5

1. Why did the computer become a film editor? It knew how to cut and paste scenes!

2. Why did the chemist become a coffee roaster? He knew the science behind the perfect roast!

3. Why did the tree become a DJ? It had the perfect balance of bass and treble!

4. Why did the math book become a surfing instructor? It understood wave equations!

5. Why did the scientist become a watchmaker? He wanted to explore the mechanics of time!

Riddly-5: The Earth's Shimmering Gems

Clue	Problem
1.	We are precious stones that form deep within the Earth's crust.
2.	We are valued for our beauty, rarity, and durability.
3.	We are used in jewelry, art, and industrial applications.
4.	We come in various colors and are formed through geological processes.
5.	What are these precious stones that form deep within the Earth's crust called?

Answer: Gemstones

Giggly-5

1. Why did the computer become an event planner? It was great at scheduling tasks!
2. Why did the chemist become a soap maker? He loved creating bubbles!
3. Why did the plant become a fashion designer? It was great at leafing through trends!
4. Why did the math book become a fortune teller? It knew how to calculate the odds!
5. Why did the scientist become a film director? He understood the science of storytelling!

Riddly-5: The Guardians of Pollination

Clue	Problem
1.	We are insects known for our role in transferring pollen from male to female flowers.
2.	We play a crucial role in plant reproduction and the production of fruits and seeds.
3.	We are known for our distinctive buzzing sound and colorful bodies.
4.	We are attracted to flowers by their nectar and collect pollen on our bodies.
5.	What are these insects known for their role in transferring pollen called?

Answer: Pollinators

Giggly-5

1. Why did the computer become a fitness trainer? It knew all about crunching numbers and abs!
2. Why did the chemist become a perfume maker? He had a nose for aromatic reactions!
3. Why did the plant start a meditation center? It knew the art of stillness!
4. Why did the math book become a traffic cop? It was great at calculating speed!
5. Why did the scientist become a music producer? He understood the sound waves!

Ignite your Intellect: Books for Smart Kids

Other Books in this series

Brainteasers & Bafflers: A Curious Collection of Riddles and Interesting Facts to Challenge Your Mind

Embark on a thrilling journey of wit and wisdom with 'Brainteasers & Bafflers'! Packed with mind-bending riddles and intriguing facts, this compendium will delight curious minds and puzzle enthusiasts alike. Unleash your inner detective and delve into a world of intellectual challenges, quirky trivia, and endless fun!

Ignite your Intellect: Books for Smart Kids

Other Books in this series

Skills for Life: The Ultimate Guide for Smart Kids to Succeed!

This book is designed to help kids between the ages of 8 and 12 develop the essential life skills they need to succeed in the modern world. From managing emotions to communicating effectively, each Chapter provides practical tips and Examples to help kids understand the importance of each skill and how to develop it effectively. We believe that these 11 essential life skills will help kids become confident, adaptable, and resilient individuals who are ready to tackle any challenge that comes their way. So, let's get started on this exciting journey of growth and development!

Printed in Great Britain
by Amazon